EUNICE ALLOH

BREAK NEGATIVE *Cycles*

Defy Mental Health Challenges by Mastering your Subconscious

INTRODUCTION.

Towards the end of the year 2019, there was a global pandemic which impacted many businesses, individuals and companies that had been established over many decades. Sadly, there were many families with individuals who were either furloughed or made redundant and others who lost loved ones without being able to say goodbye.

Since the COVID-19 pandemic was unexpected, many countries and government bodies across the globe were uncertain on how to deal with the aftermath or effectively contain and reduce the spread of the VIRUS. Consequently, some mistakes were made and there were more deaths in some countries than others. Irrespective of the surprise element of the pandemic, there was one thing that it certainly highlighted across the globe. The one thing was the importance of Mental Health & Health-Care Services across the globe.

There are many things which we humans take for granted on a daily basis and rarely give much attention to unless we are challenged to do so. Some of these things include: human contact, access to 24hrs gyms, going to the pub, going to watch football games, going to the grocery store, getting a massage, seeing loved ones etc. Yet we have been confined to our homes and not been able to freely access some of these things or maintain the luxurious lifestyles some were accustomed to. This has emphasised the importance of self-care particularly in relation to our mental health and psychological well-being.

Whilst there were many who experienced financial hardships including mental health and psychological challenges due to the pandemic, there were also others who did not as they actually obtained other financial opportunities and were able to expand their businesses into other E-Commerce avenues.

Now my question to you is this, **why did some industries, individuals, countries and small businesses experience massive fallout from the same unplanned pandemic whilst others did not**? Whatever your response is, in some cases, it will certainly be along the lines of their approach to problem solving and their ability to plan and adjust in uncertain times.

With the above response in mind, consider this: what was your approach to your self-care routine including your mental health, emotional and psychological well-being over the years and especially over the pandemic period? Would you have benefited from a better routine in ensuring that you were better equipped for the pandemic season or any future occurrences?

I do hope you responded YES! to the above question because even if your routine was splendid, to ensure that you are able to maintain and sustain it, you would have to consciously problem solve and plan how to handle and/or respond to events and situations, in order to maintain an effective mental health and psychological well-being.

That is why I decided to write this book and created the R.I.P.E. programme, to assist you in developing and maintaining a healthy mental health and psychological well-being.

As a therapist, dealing with mental health, emotional and psychological well-being issues is a norm in my practice. Yet this pandemic period has created a siege across the globe and impacted many individuals, who do not have the luxury of being able to afford private counselling and/or therapy without having to go through the National Health Service (NHS).

With most surgeries and procedures in the UK halted as a result of the pandemic, the waiting list for accessing Medical Health Service has escalated due to a shortage of healthcare workers and a backlog of cases to be attended to. In addition to this, the waiting list for Mental Health Services have increased to the point where "new clients have to wait up to 36 months" in order to be assessed to gain access to mental health and psychological services on the NHS. As ridiculous as that is, it is the unfortunate reality of many, who do not have the luxury of accessing a therapist or counsellor privately.

Hence, I decided to create this R.I.P.E. programme and book, to guide and assist you with looking after your mental health and psychological well-being in just 4 steps. My aim is to help you develop good habits and insight into yourself, so you can protect your mental health and psychological well-being, without allowing it to deteriorate. It is my desire that just as you take a sip of water and/or drink, without further thought and do it just because you want to or feel like it, you will develop the habit of mastering your subconscious so you can protect your mental health and psychological well-being.

Thank You
to All the
Amazing
People
Working
Hard
Taking Care
of Us
and
Saving
Lives.

THE R.I.P.E. APPROACH.

The ripe approach is based on the concepts of nature, i.e. fruits, plants and crops etc.
I feel this concept best explains how the human brain works.
Hence, I have deliberately chosen this concept, in relation to mental health & psychological difficulties.
I believe it provides a great illustration of how to gain insight into your thoughts and learn to begin mastering yourself!

WHAT R.I.P.E. STANDS FOR & MY 4 STEPS.

As previously stated, this programme is centred around the agricultural process, and how plants, fruits and crops, blossom or ripen when they are ready to eat or in season.

For the purpose of my focus in addressing MENTAL HEALTH & PSYCHOLOGICAL ISSUES, I have chosen to abbreviate the word **R.I.P.E.** into four steps. These four steps below, will serve as chapters in this book. Each step will demonstrate how you can begin mastering your thoughts & break the cycle of mental health.

- **R** -Recognise
- **I** - Investigate
- **P** -Prune
- **E** -Evaluate

I hope you find these steps straight forward & easy to follow. To assist on your journey to mastering your subconscious, each step will always begin with a dictionary definition of the KEY word, and some background on why it is a necessary process.

Alright let's begin!

Get ready to take charge of your Mind and change the course of your life!

Get ready to break the cycle of failure and/or rejection in your life,
so you can achieve your Personal and Professional Goals.

Get ready to break the cycle of over spending, learn to
manage your finances and maximise your resources!

Get ready to break the cycle of toxic relationships in your life.

Get ready to identify limiting beliefs and break cycles of emotional
roller coasters, so you can live your desired life!

Get ready to control and regulate your subconscious
so you can thrive in all areas of your Life.

Get ready to see yourself in a different Light!

Get ready to revolutionise your Life and create endless Possibilities!

Get ready to identify and break every limiting belief,
preventing you from starting that business!

Get ready to Unleash Yourself to Dream and Arise to your full Potential!

ONE VOICE THERAPY

LIBERATED FROM LIMITS TO YOUR INFINITE POTENTIAL

CHAPTER ONE - KNOWING YOURSELF & RECOGNISING YOUR TRIGGERS.

Ben Carson once said, "we've been conditioned to think that only politicians can solve our problems, but at some point, maybe we will wake up and recognise that it was politicians who created our problems".

The above quote will mean different things to different people but in relation to your mental health and psychological well-being, it is vital that you wake-up and realise that you are not as helpless as you think. Rather, you can actually learn to rewire your brain and condition yourself to master your subconscious, so you can break the cycle of mental health and psychological issues in your life.

To achieve this it is vital that you become an expert of yourself and know who you truly are at your core, without constantly blaming others for the state of your mental, emotional and psychological well-being.

Today, most of us have relinquished our personal power and autonomy of our lives over to politicians, the government and others as reflected in the opening quote. To reverse this process and recondition your mind, you have to take charge and decide to navigate your own life.

With that in mind, let's talk about you and your mental health, emotional and psychological well-being.

Get ready to take charge and restructure your brain!

STEP 1: RECOGNITION.

What does it mean to recognise?

- To perceive as existing or true.
- To identify as something, or someone previously seen, known.
- To accept or acknowledge something.

The above Cambridge definition informs us that it is possible for something to exist, without you being aware that it is for one reason or the other. Hence, this leads to my next question below.

Why do we not recognise things?

- We are comfortable with it.
- We have become used to them and see them as normal.
- We don't see anything wrong with them.
- We think others have a problem and there is nothing wrong with us or what we are doing!

Failure to recognise things, makes it difficult to fix and address some of the ongoing issues they cause. That is why farmers pay particular attention to their crops and spend time nurturing each one.

What do you want to notice or recognise?

- Thoughts.
- Emotions.
- Behaviour.

- Situations.
- Events.

When it comes to mastering your subconscious and preventing mental health issues, these five things are vital. Hence, in the next step, we will discuss what you do with what you have noticed or recognised about yourself, in relation to your thoughts, emotions, behaviour, events and situations.

GUIDE TO RECOGNITION.

Before going into the next chapter and step, I wanted to give you some examples that will make this first step of recognition easier. I know there are some of you reading this, who may find this recognition process very easy and others who may find it difficult to do. There might even be some wondering what I mean by recognising your triggers i.e. thoughts, emotions, actions, situations and/or events.

I can even picture some of you saying "it's impossible to know everything that goes through your mind at any given time, let alone learning to identify your emotions, behaviours, situations and/or events as well". Don't worry because I have got you covered, hence the section on examples.

It is important to note that, with practice it is possible to recognise your triggers and learn to master them. Whether you are aware of your triggers or not, they still exist and can become problematic for you, if you do not learn to recognise and manage them effectively as the farmer does with each crop.

These examples are generic and are meant to serve as a guide to recognising your own triggers in the form of thoughts, emotions, behaviours, situations and events. Should you find some of the examples below applicable to you, make a note of them and identify more personal triggers, to increase your ability to maintain a healthy mental health and psychological well-being.

EXAMPLES OF TRIGGERS.

Examples of problematic Thoughts:

- "I am not apologising first, they have to because they were wrong!".
- "I should have told them about themselves and let them have it".
- "I can't let it go because if I do, they will do it again and think it's ok".
- "I am not going to get that job, so there is no point trying or wasting my time, there are others more qualified and better than me".
- "I can pay it off next month, it's not a big deal"
- "I can just get another credit card and transfer the interest".

Examples of problematic Emotions:

- Joy.
- Excitement.
- Boredom.
- Sadness.
- Grief.
- Happiness.
- Surprise.
- Shock.
- Fear.
- Anxious.
- Greed.
- Love.
- Envy.
- Disdain.
- Disappointment.
- Disgust etc.

EXAMPLES OF TRIGGERS.

Examples of problematic Behaviours/Actions:

- Being a people pleaser saying yes to things when you should say no and vice-versa.
- Buying things you don't need in the spare of the moment and over spending etc.
- Borrowing either excessive or small amounts from various people and companies.
- Burying your head in the sand and refusing to deal with problems or waiting for permission from others before acting or making decisions.
- Jumping from one relationship straight into another.
- Staying at home and refusing to leave the house without others.
- Having emotional outbursts and constantly arguing with others.
- Only going to the shop at particular times in the day.
- Self-harming and putting yourself down etc.

Examples of problematic Situations & Events:

- Invitation to events or being on your own at home.
- Being stuck in traffic or a crowded place with others.
- Losing your job or starting a new job.
- Starting relationships, ending old ones or meeting new people.
- Being indoors or going outdoors to public places.
- Family gatherings or reunion events.
- Seeing a child or adult disrespect their parents or another.
- Someone talking over/about you or looking at you.
- Being complemented by others.
- Losing your phone or personal belongings.

I do hope that the above examples have been helpful and served as clues to what you will need to be recognising within yourself. Additionally, for those that might have been wondering where to start from and how do you go about recognising these triggers, I hope these examples have been a helpful starting point, to learning to master your subconscious.

Since you are going through this programme in your own time and pace, I would like to invite you to pause here and after each chapter, so you can go through each step and thoroughly identify your own triggers, before proceeding to the next chapter and step. Even if you have already begun the process by making notes as you were reading, I strongly urge you to still take a break and pause here and after each chapter, so you can reflect on what you have learnt about yourself thus far.

Remember that the reason you are reading this book and going through this programme, is to develop and maintain a healthy mental health and psychological well-being. Hence it is important that you get into the habit of looking after yourself and listening to your body, so you do not exhaust yourself either physically, emotionally or psychologically.

OVERVIEW.

As a reminder in Chapter 1, we looked at the first step to maintaining a healthy mental health and psychological well-being, which was to Recognise your triggers!

We noted that there are different types of triggers and highlighted that they could be a combination of Thoughts; Emotions; Behaviours; Situations and/or Events.

In the next Chapter, we are going to discuss the next step which is the investigative stage. We will be discussing the value of investigations in relation to agriculture etc and how it links with your mental health and psychological well-being.

Therefore, it is essential that you have your list of personal triggers that you identified in Step 1 nearby, so you can refer to these throughout without unnecessary distractions.

(END OF CHAPTER ONE - TAKE A BREAK).

ONE VOICE THERAPY

LIBERATED FROM LIMITS TO YOUR INFINITE POTENTIAL

CHAPTER TWO - INVESTIGATION OF YOUR TRIGGERS.

"When everything is moving and shifting, the only way to counteract chaos is stillness. When things feel extraordinary, strive for the ordinary. When the surface is wavy, dive deeper for quieter waters... and sometimes all it takes is a subtle shift in perspective, an opening of the mind, an intentional pause and reset, or a new route to start to see new options and possibilities". **Kristin Armstrong.**

Like our thoughts and triggers, most things in life are constantly changing and evolving with time. That is why researchers are constantly conducting experiments and updating their material to stay relevant. Nonetheless, farmers and those in the field of agriculture are also constantly doing the same. Through their investigations, farmers have been able to invent new ways of growing crops in greenhouses and artificially manufacture produce in unnatural terrains and climates.

Consequently, in order to become an expert of yourself and master your subconscious, you have to develop the act of patience and being tenacious, to ensure that you can change your perspective and intentionally open your mind, in order to reset your brain and break the cycle of mental health and psychological issues in your life and that of the next generation!

Now sit comfortably and let's continue.

STEP 2: INVESTIGATION.

What does it mean to Investigate?

- To examine or study.
- To inquire systemically.
- To search or examine into particulars.
- To examine in detail.

Similarly, these definitions (Merriam Webster) above demonstrate that embarking on an investigation, requires the gathering of information to solve a problem(s).

Just as a farmer will carefully inspect & investigate each crop to check the progress of its growth, the investigation of your thoughts, emotions, behaviour, situations and events have got to become a gradual and daily process, so you can break the cycle of MENTAL and/or PSYCHOLOGICAL issues in your life!

Why do we investigate things?

- To attempt to learn the facts about something.
- To uncover something hidden or unique.
- To understand something complex.
- To find a motive or cause for something.

When done correctly, it is during the investigative process that farmers or police officers acquire the most accurate and relevant information necessary to solve the mystery they are presented with.

Likewise, to break the cycle of MENTAL, EMOTIONAL & PSYCHOLOGICAL difficulties, you have to continually inspect your thoughts, emotions, situations, behaviour & events.

To assist you with the investigation process, I have generated a list of questions below, to help with your mastery journey. Answering these questions will lead you into the pruning process discussed in step 3.

Before we delve straight into the questions generated to assist you with this step, let's first discuss the importance of conducting investigations.

Outcomes and the importance of Investigations.

From our definitions at the start, we discover that conducting an investigation allows us to gather and assess the information we have and gain answers to puzzling questions. We also learnt from our opening quote by **Kristin Armstrong** that, investigations provide us with clarity, a fresh perspective of things, "opens the mind, helps to see new options and possibilities" that would otherwise be missed. Unlike farmers, we do not intentionally pause to examine our crops (ourselves) so we can encourage positive growth, in this case a healthy and positive mental health and psychological well-being.

Similarly, many of you reading this book would have either had a job interview at some point in your life, been in the process of looking for a job or even been in search of new employees to either manage your teams or provide particular services. Just as you conduct thorough background searches on individuals and/or companies, to ensure their values match yours and the needs required, it is essential that you adopt this same investigative process with yourself particularly in relation to your mental health, emotional and psychological well-being. Otherwise, you will find yourself in a constant mental and psychological battle, which could become detrimental to all aspects of your life and well-being.

Great! Now with that in mind I encourage you to grab a book preferably the one you used in step 1 when identifying your triggers. Additionally, you can grab your ipad, a phone, recorder or whatever device works best for you and your learning style, as you will need these when going through the questions below.

Whatever your learning style, I strongly recommend that you take note of your responses to these questions, in relation to the triggers you identified in step 1. You can do so by either writing or recording your responses so you can return to them and continue evaluating these in the final step which we will discuss later. I know there might be some of you thinking "I can just do these in my head and don't have to write these down", trust me as great as your memory might be, that will not be the best thing to do as you go through this programme, so please find a creative way to record your responses.

QUESTIONS TO CONSIDER IN STEP 2.

- **How realistic or helpful are my thoughts, emotions or behaviour?**

- **What can I do about this situation or event?**

- **Why do I feel this particular way?**

- **When did I first notice this thought, emotion or behaviour?**

- **How did I respond in that situation or event?**

- **Where did I learn to behave, think or feel like this?**

- **Why should I change my thinking and how I see things?**

These questions are just a starting point, to encourage you to examine your thought process. They are by no means an exclusive list, so generate some additional questions on your own, using the above as a guide, to ensure that you effectively conduct the investigative process of examining the thoughts, emotions, behaviour, situations and events linked to the mental, emotional and psychological difficulties you experience.

Being totally honest with yourself when answering these questions, will be the success of your liberation and ability to complete the pruning process in the next step.

OVERVIEW.

As easy and straightforward as the investigative process seems, any farmer, researcher and/ or police officer, will honestly tell you that it can sometimes be the most difficult process after you recognise that something needs to change or a crime has been committed.

One of the reasons why it can sometimes be the most difficult and longest processes, is because it requires you to gather, verify and compare the information and/or evidence you already have to existing or new ones, in order to challenge your thinking and change perspectives or direction, to ensure that you achieve the correct outcomes.

Likewise as we did in chapter 1, I would like to remind you to go through this stage carefully, using the questions provided and your own ones, to allow you to effectively challenge the thoughts linked to each of your identified triggers. For some of you, the questions provided on the previous page will be enough and for others, you may require additional one-to-one support in therapy at a later stage. Whatever category you fall into, I am happy to assist should you wish to proceed at a later stage.

(END OF CHAPTER TWO - TAKE ANOTHER MENTAL BREAK & REFLECT)!

ONE VOICE THERAPY

LIBERATED FROM LIMITS TO YOUR INFINITE POTENTIAL

CHAPTER THREE - UNDERSTANDING YOURSELF (THE PRUNING PROCESS).

According to **Elisabeth Kubler-Ross**, "people are like stained-glass windows. They sparkle and shine when the sun is out, but when the darkness sets in, their true beauty is revealed only if there is a light from within".

Similarly, **Ben Carson** is also known to have said "it's very important for people to know themselves and understand what their value system is, because if you don't know what your value system is, then you don't know what risks are worth taking and which ones are worth avoiding".

We humans are complex creatures with a plethora of principles and belief systems that govern our lives and shape our interactions with ourselves, others and the world around us. Unfortunately, most of us are oblivious to these belief systems and how they are impacting our interactions and mental health and psychological well-being. Fortunately for you and I, we do not fall into this category, as going through this programme and making it this far has given you insight into your triggers and increased your awareness of some of these problematic beliefs. Hence, you are now equipped to take charge and know which risks to take and which ones to avoid, to ensure you maintain a healthy mental health and psychological well-being routine.

In todays' social media and celebrity obsessed culture, if you ask most people who they are, it is not a question they can honestly answer with confidence without either waffling in their response or cracking their brains to seem intelligent or interesting.

Whilst most people often answer this question "who are you?", with a list of their credentials or accolades etc, there are others who often avoid this question like a plaque, as they feel they have nothing to offer as they have no achievements etc. Hence it is my desire that, wherever you are at this point in your life, on completing this programme, you will be able to honestly answer this question with confidence without experiencing unnecessary distress.

Together with the insight that you have gained thus far in the first two steps and chapters, at the end of this programme, you will be able to truly know and understand yourself at the core, especially learning about what makes you tick, understand your values and your ability to control and master your subconscious.

Well without further ado, let's move onto step 3 on PRUNING.

STEP 3: PRUNING.

What does it mean to Prune?

Merriam Webster dictionary defines pruning as:

- To cut or lop off twigs, branches or roots.
- To remove anything considered undesirable or superfluous.

Why is pruning done or important in farming?

- To remove dead, diseased or damaged crops.
- To allow crops to grow properly, without defects.
- To promote and encourage new growth of crops.
- To prevent wrong positioning of crops and mixture with unwanted weeds.

When you speak to farmers, they will tell you that the pruning process is essential in all seasons regardless of the size of the crop. Consequently, careful and practical steps are taken, to ensure that all diseased, damaged or dead weeds are removed, to avoid contamination with the final produce. Any good farmer will also inform you that there are rules to follow, when pruning, to ensure that you do not cause damage to perfectly healthy crops and are able to retain the uniformity of growth.

Additionally, they will tell you that it is important that you take note of the damaged, diseased and/or dead crops or produce, so you can accurately point out their position in relation to the healthy ones, without mistaking them for healthy crops or losing sight of them. To ensure you accurately prune or cut off the correct branches to promote growth, without causing harm to the already healthy branches or produce!

RULES OF PRUNING.

Therefore just as farmers do, to break the cycle of mental health Issues and truly understand or know yourself:

- You have got to learn to master your subconscious, so you can remove and get rid of any **dead, diseased and damaged** belief system that you hold!

It does not matter how long or short you have held these beliefs, rather it is essential that you continue to **recognise, investigate, prune & evaluate** them, to avoid unnecessary negative repetitive cycles either in your life or that of your children and generations to come.

To help you understand and fully conduct this pruning process, we are going to discuss the rules of pruning in agriculture. According to the **University of Florida IFAS Gardening**

Solutions, there are 3 steps to follow when pruning and four rules of pruning which all farmers have to bear in mind.

These rules include:

- **Keeping it healthy** - by removing all dead, damaged and diseased branches.
- **Keeping it strong** - by removing or reducing the length of stems competing with the main leader.
- **Keeping it uniform** - by removing any branches that look out of place or cross touching each other.
- **Keep it minor** - by hiring an expert to correctly prune your trees or branches so they can withstand and resist further damage.

I am sure other farmers and sites would suggest more rules, yet for the purpose of this step and programme, we will only be focusing on the above four. Consequently, take note of these rules as you go through this step in relation to your mental health and mastering your subconscious.

ACCURACY OF PRUNING.

CAUTION:
Since you are not currently sitting before a therapist, to keep you accountable and ensure that you are accurately pruning the unhelpful beliefs, it is crucial that you do this step effectively without deceiving yourself.

Similar to the previous chapters and steps, you will need to have your notepad or whatever device you used in steps 1&2, when you identified your triggers and answered the questions in the previous step.

As we demonstrated in the previous section on the rules to pruning, farmers take particular care and follow a set of rules and steps before pruning or cutting trees. Consequently, in this step we are going to discuss how you can use the four rules previously discussed, to help with examining your responses to the questions discussed in step 2.

To do this effectively, you will need to review each question and establish your own follow-up questions, to determine whether a belief system you hold, is either completely **dead, diseased or damaged.**

For example as highlighted in the examples of triggers section in step 1, if a personal trigger of yours is "losing your phone or only leaving the house at particular times" etc, then you need to review this situation and your response to the questions in step 2, to understand the following, when this began, how long it has been going on for and what you do to manage this behaviour etc.

You may need to generate more open questions using **"what, who, where, why, how and when"** etc, to correctly identify the **diseased, damaged** and **dead** beliefs impacting your life and interaction with others. Being able to distinguish between these 3 factors, will allow you to either adjust and repair the belief or completely replace it with something new using the four rules of pruning previously discussed.

RELATING RULES OF PRUNING TO YOUR THOUGHTS.

As stated in step 1, we sometimes don't recognise things because of how comfortable and easy they make us feel. Hence, when done properly, the pruning process will not make you feel comfortable or happy with the changes you are making or considering. Rather it will make you question whether there is any point in continuing with this process.

Hence throughout this step remember these rules below:

- You can't master your subconscious if you don't replace your dead, diseased and damaged thoughts so you can keep them healthy.

- You won't be able to keep and maintain a strong mental health, emotional and psychological well-being, if you are not actively renewing your mind or aware of your thoughts and triggers.

- You can only achieve your goals and live the balanced or uniform life you want and desire, by either tweaking or completely changing those unhelpful beliefs that cross over, and are sometimes helpful yet in other cases can prove problematic.

- You don't have to change everything about your beliefs or thought process, to master your subconscious it is just those minor ones impacting your life.

Some of you may need to seek further help through therapy and counselling to effectively master your subconscious.

OVERVIEW.

I do hope you found the rules of pruning useful in relation to this step and continuing that investigative process of yourself, by cutting off or removing the problematic thoughts and/or beliefs system contributing to the mental and psychological difficulties you are either experiencing or will do in future.

Before moving on to step 4, I have outlined some signs to consider, that confirms accuracy in pruning below.

How to know I am pruning correctly:

- When you feel like giving-up with this whole process of questioning and examining your beliefs.

- When you feel uncomfortable within yourself with the changes because you are no longer in your comfort zone.

- When you start asking yourself questions like, why do I, or should I be the one to make the change and why not him/her/them?

(END OF CHAPTER THREE - TAKE ANOTHER BREAK BEFORE THE FINAL CHAPTER).

ONE VOICE THERAPY

LIBERATED FROM LIMITS TO YOUR INFINITE POTENTIAL

CHAPTER FOUR - MASTERING YOURSELF & YOUR SUBCONSCIOUS.

John Wooden said *"without proper self-evaluation, failure is inevitable"*.

According to **John Maxwell.** *"if we are growing, we are always going to be out of our comfort zone"*.

For most of you being in your comfort zone is something that comes naturally that you don't have to give much thought to. With growth comes different levels of maturity, sadly many people grow and fail to mature simply because they have not mastered the act of self-discipline, evaluation of the ability to openly give and receive constructive feedback.

Henry Cloud alleged that *"the natural response to evaluation is to feel judged. We have to mature to a place where we respond to it with gratitude and love feedback"*.

No-one likes being told that they are not the best at what they do or that there is someone out there much better than them. The truth is "Rome wasn't built in a day" as it's often said. If you desire to reach this self-actualisation state where you are completely in charge of your thoughts and able to gain mastery over your subconscious, you have got to become a student of yourself and not others as most people do.

Being able to master yourself and your subconscious is the best gift you can give yourself. This gift of self mastery must cost you something, push you towards your dreams and require you to be tenacious in striving to be the best there is, through continuous self development and learning.

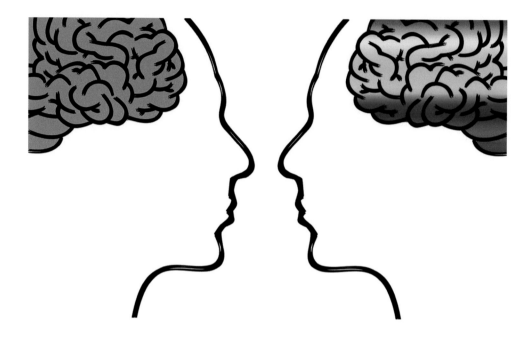

I can hear some of you asking "what has this got to do with mental health and psychological well-being?". Well I'm glad you ask as it has everything to do with your ability to maintain a healthy mental, emotional and psychological health & well-being.

I am sure you don't need me to inform you that the reason there's a rise in mental health and psychological Issues today, is because most people are struggling to manage their thoughts and are plagued with cognitive dissonance that impacts their ability to function normally. Therefore, as you go through this book and programme, it is your responsibility to ensure that you continually adopt the posture of a student, so you can effectively **R**ecognise, **I**nvestigate, **P**rune and **E**valuate every single thought you experience, so you can learn to master your subconscious and break the cycle of mental health and psychological issues in your life.

As much as I may want to give you more information on how to continue with this process of self-mastery, I am limited by what I can share with you in this book at this time. Consequently, if you would like more information or want to know how you can work with me privately, visit www.onevoicecounselling.com or https://linktr.ee/euniceperceptivecoach. Now let's move onto our final step of evaluation, which will also require you to have your notepad or whatever electronic device.

To recap below are the four steps we have learnt to mastering your subconscious:

1. Recognise your triggers.
2. Investigate the circumstances around those triggers.
3. Prune the unhelpful thoughts associated with each trigger either by removing or replacing your thoughts.
4. Evaluation of everything you identified from steps 1-3. **(Yet to discuss in this chapter).**

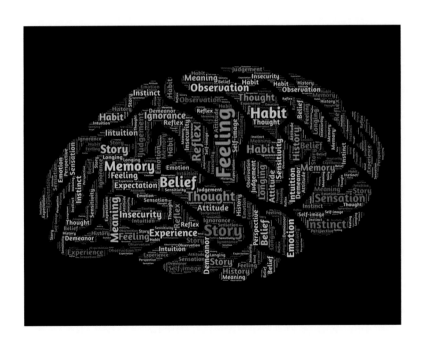

STEP 4 EVALUATION.

What does it mean to Evaluate? *(Merriam Webster dictionary definition).*

- To determine or fix value off.
- To discover the significance, worth or condition of something.
- To carefully study something through appraisal.
- To rate, value and assess the worth of a thing.

Why do we continue Evaluating things?

- To increase awareness of problems.
- To discover the growth of a thing.
- To change stance or direction.
- To identify new solutions to solving the problem.
- To identify and understand what is working and what is not.
- To provide clarity on what else needs pruning.
- To recognise effective strategies to maintain.

Both the above definitions of evaluation and why it's done, emphasise the importance of this process and step.

In her book "Hello Tomorrow! The transformational power of vision", **Cindy Trimm** wrote *"experience comes when you exercise your will to accomplish something, no matter how massive, daunting, or impossible it seems. A vision will help you to overcome the seemingly insurmountable".*

Consequently, just as a farmer carefully studies each crop, he/she identifies the diseased, damaged and/or dead ones and strategically prunes them to avoid ruining his/her vision. You will also need to continually assess the triggers i.e. (thoughts, emotions, situations, behaviours and events) in your life, by reviewing the responses to the questions discussed in Step 3.

As demonstrated in the above definitions, continuous evaluation of events, allows you to discover the significance and worth of a thing, so you can either change your stance or strategically prune anything additional that is required.

Hence, it is vital to note that all the above 4 Steps, **(Recognition, Investigation, Pruning & Evaluation)**, are essential to breaking the cycle of mental health & psychological difficulties in your life.

Attaining mastery over your thoughts and subconscious, or in the context of farming, becoming a **ripe** fruit or crop is a gradual process, so you have got to push yourself out of your comfort zone and not get complacent.

According to **Neville Goddard** *"when you attain control of the internal direction of your attention, you will no longer stand in shallow water but launch out into the deep of life"*.

Therefore I urge you to develop the act of self-evaluation, and let this become a daily habit where you constantly review all 4 Steps, throughout your interaction with yourself and others. As it is the only way that you develop and sustain any changes required to maintain a healthy mental health and psychological well-being.

Further benefits of continuous Self-Evaluation:

- Helps to identify what else is needed to completely master and challenge your beliefs system.

- Helps to increase awareness of what you are doing to sabotage your relationships.

- Helps to recognise further steps needed, to assist with pursuing and achieving your personal and/or professional goals.

- Helps to Identify additional support systems and accountability partners.

I hope you have found these 4 Steps and the R.I.P.E. Programme effective, in beginning to master your subconscious, so you can thrive and S.O.A.R. (Stand Out & Re-establish Yourself) in your life.

I do hope that I can continue to serve you, on your journey to self-development and breaking the cycle of mental health & psychological issues, through our one-to-one therapy options.

In these sessions you will get the opportunity to engage in bespoke, life changing assignments that will help you to further identify the particular thinking biases and personal rules and/or belief systems you hold within your subconscious that also contribute to various mental and psychological difficulties you experience.

To find out more about our various therapy options and/or other services, please visit our website at www.onevoicecounselling.com / https://linktr.ee/euniceperceptivecoach.

Thank you for allowing me to SERVE you!

I would like to leave you with two of my favourite quotes below.

"If you are going to reap the harvest of vision you have been planting, you must learn to expertly cultivate both your energy and your time" **- Cindy Trimm.**

"… don't let your history interfere with your destiny! Let today be the day you stop being a victim of your circumstance and start taking action towards the life you want. You have the power and time to shape your life. Break free from your poisonous victim mentality and embrace the truth of your greatness. You were not meant for a mundane or mediocre life!" **- Steve Maraboli.**

ONE VOICE THERAPY
LIBERATED FROM LIMITS TO YOUR INFINITE POTENTIAL

TODAY IS THE DAY TO BREAK THOSE LIMITING BELIEFS!

Book your Clarity Call NOW & Let's Begin.

https://calendly.com/euniceperceptivecoach/60min

Let's rejuvenate your life Now.

Break those Psychological Barriers Now.

Make this your Breakthrough Year, where you achieve all your Personal & Professional Goals to S.O.A.R into your future!

ONE VOICE THERAPY
LIBERATED FROM LIMITS TO YOUR INFINITE POTENTIAL

HOW TO CONTACT US:

Visit our Web addresses:

www.onevoicecounselling.com / https://linktr.ee/euniceperceptivecoach.

Email US:

info.victoriouswomen@gmail.com / euniceperceptivecoach@gmail.com.

Social Media Handles:

Follow us on **Instagram** @euniceperceptivecoach.

Follow us on **Twitter** @perceptivecoach.

Follow us on **Facebook** @perceptivecoacheunice.

Follow us on **LinkedIn** @euniceperceptivecoach.

Follow us on **You-tube** @eunice perceptive coach.

I look forward to hearing from you soon and serving you further, to gain total mastery over your subconscious thoughts!

ONE VOICE THERAPY

LIBERATED FROM LIMITS TO YOUR INFINITE POTENTIAL

ONE VOICE THERAPY

LIBERATED FROM LIMITS TO YOUR INFINITE POTENTIAL

References & Bibliographies:

Ben Carson - "it's very important for people to know themselves..." https://quotefancy. com/quote/954055/Ben-Carson-It-s-very-important-for-people-to-know-themselves-and-understand-what-their.

Ben Carson - "we have been conditioned to think only..." https://www.facebook.com/ FoxBusiness/posts/weve-been-conditioned-to-think-that-only-politicians-can-solve-our-problems-but-/10153892947535238/

Cindy Trimm - Hello, Tomorrow - The Transformational Power of Vision.

Cambridge dictionary - recognition https://dictionary.cambridge.org/

Elizabeth Kubler-Ross -"people are like stained glass..." https://www.goodreads.com/ quotes/6826-people-are-like-stained-glass-windows-they-sparkle-and-shine-when.

https://www.merriam-webster.com/dictionary/

Henry Cloud - "The natural response to evaluation..." https://www.azquotes.com/quotes/ topics/evaluation.html

John Wooden - "Without proper self-evaluation..." https://www.azquotes.com/quotes/topics/evaluation.html

John C. Maxwell - "if we are growing, we are always..." https://www.goodreads.com/ quotes/38432-if-we-are-growing-we-are-always-going-to-be

Kristian Armstrong "when everything is moving... sometimes all it takes is a subtle change"... https://regoslife.com/tag/kristin-armstrong-quotes/ https://www.goodreads.com/author/ quotes/41072.Kristin_Armstrong.

Neville Goddard "when you attain control of the internal..." https://www.azquotes.com/quote/879691

Steve Maraboli - "Today is a new day!..."
https://www.goodreads.com/quotes/416919-today-is-a-new-day-don-t-let-your-history-interfere

T.D. Jakes - SOAR - Build your Vision from the ground Up.

UF|IFAS Gardening Solutions. University of Florida - https://gardeningsolutions.ifas.ufl.edu/care/pruning/pruning-three-steps.html.

EPILOGUE

Watch out for my forthcoming books below:

RESPECT

LOVE

GUILT & SHAME.

Please remember to send me an email and request your FREE copy of my SOAR guide! (Part 1 of our growth series).

Use the details below to get in touch for your FREE gift.

euniceperceptivecoach@gmail.com

ONE VOICE THERAPY
LIBERATED FROM LIMITS TO YOUR INFINITE POTENTIAL

ONE VOICE THERAPY

LIBERATED FROM LIMITS TO YOUR INFINITE POTENTIAL

ACKNOWLEDGEMENTS

**Firstly, I thank God for the idea, ability and
title of this book and programme!**

Next I would like to thank all my book testers:

Kojo Ofori, Magnus Alloh, Charlotte Melfah, Landi Oshinowo,
Lara Jonah, Paul Bessitch, Luciana Alloh, Tina Divine, Esther
Danquah, Chioma Obi, Megan Alloh and Liam Alloh.

Thank you all for making time out of your busy schedules to read this book
and provide me with feedback on how it can be made exceptional.

**I really appreciate your feedback and value
your input in my life and this book!**

Thank you all from the depths of my heart.

ONE VOICE THERAPY
LIBERATED FROM LIMITS TO YOUR INFINITE POTENTIAL